WHISPERINGS

Bible stories proclaiming
the great name, Jesus

Written by Yeonjai Rah

Illustrated by Mary D. Black

Copyright © 2013 Yeonjai Rah

All rights reserved.

ISBN-10:0989917800
ISBN-13:978-0-9899178-0-3

Scripture quotations, unless otherwise indicated, are taken from the New American Standard Bible®,Copyright © 1960, 1962, 1963, 1968, 1971, 1972, 1973,1975, 1977, 1995 by The Lockman Foundation Used by permission." (www.Lockman.org)

Italics in Scripture quotations reflect the author's added emphasis.

Cover design and Illustration by Mary D. Black

All rights reserved. No part of this book may be reproduced or transmitted in any form or by any means, electronic or mechanical, including photocopying and recording, or by any information storage and retrieval system, without permission in writing from the author.

DEDICATION

To the teachers and volunteers of Friendship International
at First Baptist Church at Round Rock, Texas

ACKNOWLEDGEMENTS

Kathy Nichols, for her mentoring and editing
Mary D. Black, for her wonderful illustrations
Brenda Brinkley, for encouraging me to publish this book
Linda Stevenson and *Donna Baird*, for praying with me.
Shangmin Choi, who always encourages me to write

Most of the contents of this book were originally weekly devotionals that the author shared for Friendship International.

FOREWORD

Photographic technology has come a long way over the years. What began as an interesting novelty over a century ago has today become an integral part of our lives as we are bombarded with images on a daily, even an hourly basis. It is hard to imagine a world without pictures.

In the time in which the Bible was written, it was a world without pictures. There were no digital cameras and cell phones. There was no photographic documentation of the most important story in all of history; the coming of God in the flesh into this world.

What did He look like? Artists have painted portraits of Jesus in a way that strikes the fires our imagination and places within our minds an image of our Lord. But we have no actual picture of Jesus anywhere.

If you look carefully, however, you will see the face of Jesus' on every page of the Bible. His image permeates the scriptures, inspired by the Holy Spirit, in every story, every verse, every sentence. With an acuity that surpasses even the most advanced digital technology we have today, the Bible burns into our minds a vision of a loving Savior Who came into our world to show us God.

Whisperings begins with the faith statement that "Jesus is the center of the Bible." With the skill of a true wordsmith, Yeonjai Rah helps us to "see" those pictures of Jesus that are so vividly given to us in His word. She offers us a vision of His face in both the Old and New Testament stories. Her love for the Lord and her faith in the scriptures are evident as she helps to bring alive the story of Jesus' love which is so evident throughout the Bible.

Mary Black is a gifted artist who has blessed countless people with her abilities. God has given her an incredible gift. To further spark our imaginations, she uses her skill to illustrate Whisperings with a gallery of beautiful images that touches both the mind and the heart.

Whisperings will bless you and bring the presence of Jesus Christ alive as you read each page. Yeonjai and Mary have given us a gift that is both unique and filled with the wonder of faith in Jesus Christ.

You will be blessed.

Gary Lynn Brinkley,
Senior Pastor,
First Baptist Church at Round Rock (www.fbcrr.org)

CONTENTS

FOREWORD v

PREFACE x

1 THE LIGHT 1

2 THE TREE OF LIFE 5

3 THE LEATHER COAT 9

4 LAW AND GRACE 13

5 LIVING WATER 17

6 THE LAMB 21

7 BONE OF MY BONES 23

8 ADAM'S FAILURE AND JESUS' VICTORY 25

9 TEMPTATION 29

10 THE LADDER 33

11 THE SEED 39

12 ANOINTED KING 43

13 ANOINTED PROPHET 47

14 ANOINTED PRIEST	51
15 SARAH AND MARY	53
16 ISAAC	57
17 ISAAC VS. ISHMAEL	63
18 EARLY IN THE MORNIG	67
19 CALL ON THE NAME OF THE LORD	69
20 HERE I AM	73
21 BROAD PATH OR NARROW PATH	77
22 FROM THE CAVE	81
23 FREEDOM	85
24 JOSEPH	89
25 GIVE THANKS	93
26 UP TO THE BRIM	97
ABOUT THE AUTHOR	103
ABOUT THE ILLUSTRATOR	103

WHISPERINGS

PREFACE

Jesus is the pivotal story in God's revelation, the story that gathers all the other stories into its orbit, establishes the center, and provides the comprehensive coherence. [Eugene Peterson (1997). Leap Over a Wall, p. 6]

Jesus is the center of the Bible. I believe that every story in the Bible revolves around the story of Jesus. The stories of Adam and Eve, Noah, Abraham, Isaac, Jacob, Joseph, and David are like the planets in the solar system and Jesus' story is the sun. Planets do not have their own lights. They shine in the dark night because they reflect the sun's light. Like this, other stories in the Bible can be properly interpreted through the light of Jesus' story. Other stories are access points to Jesus' story, which is huge and great, beyond human comprehension.

If you ever tried a book called "Where's Waldo?", you probably know the thrill when you find him. I felt the same way. You won't find the name Jesus in the Old Testament. However, His name is all over the stories in the Bible. When you walk into the garden called the Bible, every single leaf that reflects light in the spring breeze is whispering the name of Jesus. Every single rock on the ground and cloud in the sky sing His name. I found that everything in the Bible eventually points toward Him.

My life story, which used to be a wandering meteor, is now settled in the orbit of Jesus' story. I hope my life reflects His light and can be understood and interpreted in His light, and serves to point others to the greatest story of God.

Yeonjai Rah
April, 2014

YEONJAI RAH

Whisperings

Bible Stories proclaiming
the Greatest Name, Jesus

1 THE LIGHT

> "In the beginning God created the heavens and the earth.
> The earth was formless and void, and darkness was over the surface of the deep, and the Spirit of God was moving over the surface of the waters.
> Then God said, 'Let there be light' and there was light."
> (Genesis 1:1-3)

I vividly remember the first time I opened the Bible. It was a thick book and the pages were so thin. I did not know where to start reading. So, I started at the beginning; Genesis 1:1, "In the beginning God created the heavens and the earth." And the second verse read, "The earth was formless and void, empty, and darkness was over the surface of the deep, and the Spirit of God was moving over the surface of the waters."

The words, formless, empty, and dark sounded sad to me. With no light and no life, it sounded like the earth was helpless and hopeless. So I read the next verse: "Then God said, 'Let there be light'; and there was light." It wasn't until verse 3 that God gave light to the earth. I wondered, "Why didn't God make the light first and then the earth? Why did the earth spend time without the light -- formless, empty, and dark?"

After several weeks had passed since I began to go to church,

God showed me a vision. I saw a very dark creature sitting curled up in a corner of a dark street. The creature had no eyes, mouth, or nose— nothing. It was neither an animal nor a person. It was just something. The creature seemed to have deep sorrow and emptiness. It wanted to cry out, but could make no sound for it had no mouth. But then, I saw a figure of light coming toward the creature.

In the vision, the figure had the shape of Jesus–full of light – and a brilliant light was shining all about him. The figure of light came to the creature, hugged it and said "Yeonjai, Yeonjai, cry as much as you want" and then suddenly the creature burst out crying. The creature cried until it had poured out all the tears in its heart. As the creature cried, I knew it was my soul crying. I felt ultimate peace, a greater peace than I felt at my mother's bosom. And the creature thought, "I am filthy, literally, full of dirt and Jesus is so clean and white, so full of light."

Whenever I read Genesis 1:1-3, I remember the vision God showed me, almost twenty years ago. God allowed me to spend some of my life without the Light so that I would realize how hopeless and helpless I was without Jesus. That day God said to me "let there be light." Since then Jesus has been my Light.

WHISPERINGS

YEONJAI RAH

2 THE TREE OF LIFE

*The LORD God planted a garden toward the east, in Eden;
and there He placed the man whom He had formed.
Out of the ground the LORD God caused to grow every tree
that is pleasing to the sight and good for food;
the tree of life also in the midst of the garden,
and the tree of the knowledge of good and evil. (Genesis 2:8-9)*

In Genesis Chapter 2, I see God as a Gardner. Jesus also said "My Father is the Gardner" in John 15:1 (NIV). The first garden He made on the earth was Eden. God made this garden for His precious children. The environment was perfect. The woman did not need to go grocery shopping, cook or wash dishes, and do laundry. Adam and Eve simply ate fruit from all kinds of trees. Everything was organic! Adam did not work for food because God had provided their food. Adam took care of the animals. That was his job. And Eve helped him. That was her job.

God put two trees in the middle of the garden: one was called the Tree of Life and the other was called – a little bit longer name – the Tree of Knowledge of Good and Evil! God told Adam, "You will surely die if you eat fruit from the Tree of the Knowledge of Good and Evil." Unfortunately, Adam and Eve chose to eat from the forbidden tree, not from the Tree of Life. They did not take God's word seriously, that they would "surely die". The result of their choice was exactly what God said. They died. They did not die physically on the spot. But their death started on the day Adam and Eve trusted themselves more than God. Death became part of their lives.

After they ate from the forbidden tree, Adam and Eve covered their bodies with fig leaves because they felt shame. They also hid from God and became afraid of Him and they blamed others. Adam told God "because of the woman *You* put here" and Eve said "because of the serpent." Blaming is a sin we can find in our daily lives. Here are examples. If you have ever watched a Korean drama, then you have seen a woman yelling to her son "You're just like *Your* father." She never says, "You are like *My* husband!" Fortune tellers say, "Your life has problems because of your birth date, and where you live." Psychologists blame the way your parents raised you and sociologists blame the schools and society. The blaming goes on and on. I blamed my spouse, parents, my society, and even God if something wrong happened to me.

I thought I could cover my weakness and shame with what I made or bought. While a teenager, I used expensive shoes, fancy bags and clothes as my cover. When a little older, I thought my education, social status, achievements and my own righteousness could cover me and make me look better. But all these things were like fig leaves-temporal and perishable, and unworthy before the eyes of God. And I wanted to hide from Him. The image of God I had before I believed in Jesus was like a judge searching for my faults.

Besides blame, shame and fear, more things were in the "Death Package" in Adam and Eve's life: hard work, pain, inequity, labor to grow food, and finally physical death. But gracious God put another tree in the middle of Garden: The Tree of Life. This tree is the only way to wash away the poison of our disobedience.

Jesus said "I am the true vine and the Father is the Gardener and you are branches" and in Him is life (John 15:1). Tree of Life foreshadows Jesus as the only way a person can overcome the power of Death. Jesus said if anyone does not remain in Him that person is like a branch that is thrown away and dries up. Such branches are picked up, thrown into the fire and burned. These words reminded me that God told Adam, "You will surely die." However, Jesus, the Tree of Life, is inviting us to "Remain in Me, and I will remain in you. No branch can bear fruit by itself; it must remain in the vine. Apart from Me you can do nothing."

Here, in the middle of my life and your life, God has put two trees: The Tree of Life and The Tree of Knowledge of Good and Evil. I am not asking which tree we will choose because we have already chosen the second one when we sinned, and then came under the power of death. Let's turn toward our one and only hope, Jesus! When I became a branch of the Tree of Life, I started to taste the Package of Life: love, joy, forgiveness, peace, patience, and more. Do you know what the final element in the package of life is? It is Eternal Life. "God loves the world so much that whoever believes in Jesus shall not perish but have eternal life"(John 3:16).

3 THE LEATHER COAT

> The LORD God made garments of skin
> for Adam and his wife, and clothed them.
> (Genesis 3:21)

In Genesis 1 God is the Creator, and in Genesis 2 He is the Gardener. Now in Genesis 3, God is the Clothes-maker. In chapter two I talked about the Package of Death. One of the elements in the package was shame. Adam and Eve made coverings with fig leaves to cover their shame. However, fig leaves are weak, temporal and perishable. After Adam and Eve did not take God's commands seriously and ate from the forbidden tree, they were not able to live in the beautiful garden anymore. But before God sent them away from the garden, He gave them a gift. He made clothing for them out of leather, the skin of animals. How strong and long-lasting leather is, especially compared to fig leaves!

Let's think about where the leather came from. From an animal of course. But to get skin to make leather, the animal must first be killed. Now think of the Garden of Eden. There was no death so far. Adam and Eve and animals had never experienced any kind of death before the man and woman sinned. They may have had no idea what death was. In Eden, there was not even "natural" death from aging. Do you remember what Adam's job was? He took care of the animals. Adam and Eve received leather clothing from an innocent animal, perhaps one that Adam and Eve had loved and taken care of. Can you imagine how shocking it was for Adam and Eve to witness one of their animals being killed to give them long-lasting garments? If I had been Adam, I would have felt sorry and wept over the clothes.

I believe that through the leather clothing, God wanted to tell Adam and Eve what Jesus, the Lamb of God, would do for them. God's innocent One died on the cross, for what? To cover us with His righteousness, the long-lasting and eternal covering. The fig leaves of our own righteousness and efforts can never cover our shame. If we deeply realize the meaning of the death of Jesus on the Cross, we should be greatly shocked. The Son of God, who never sinned, had to sacrifice His life for us. In the Bible I found verses that say Jesus is like clothing: "Put on the Lord Jesus Christ" (Romans 13:14a) and "For all of you who were baptized into Christ have clothed yourselves with Christ" (Galatians 3:27).

What do you wear? Fig-leaf coverings that you made? Or, leather clothing God made? Would you like to wear the garment made by the best Clothing-Maker in the Universe? You will have not just a life-time warranty, but an eternal life-time warranty!

4 LAW AND GRACE

*But from the tree of the knowledge of good and evil you shall not eat,
for in the day that you eat from it you will surely die.
(Genesis 2:17)*

*What shall we say then? Is the Law sin? May it never be! On the contrary,
I would not have come to know sin except through the Law
(Romans 7:7a)*

*and this commandment, which was to result in life,
proved to result in death for me
(Romans 7:10).*

Why did God put the Tree of Knowledge of Good and Evil in the perfect garden? If God hadn't put that tree in the garden, Adam and Eve would not have sinned, and then the world would still be a paradise! This thought oozed out of my brains one day. Many people might wonder, like me, why God unnecessarily caused problems by putting the Tree of Knowledge of Good and Evil in His perfect garden. Why didn't God plant only the Tree of Life? Well, if the Tree of Knowledge of Good and Evil was necessary in His Garden, God would put it somewhere at the margins of Eden, not in the center next to the Tree of Life.

I also wondered why God named the tree "Tree of the Knowledge of Good and Evil." Why didn't God name it "Tree of Death"? Isn't it a good contrast, and short: Tree of Life and Tree of Death? But God chose the long and inconvenient name: the Tree of the Knowledge of Good and Evil.

Some of my curiosity was answered when I was reading the book of Romans. I found some similarities between the Law and the Tree of Knowledge of Good and Evil. Paul contrasts two different sources of righteousness; keeping the Law and having faith in Christ. First, both the Law and the Tree by themselves are good. Knowing Good and Evil itself is not an evil thing at all. In fact, this knowledge is an attribute of God "Behold, the man has become like one of Us, knowing good and evil" (Genesis 3: 22). What is the main purpose of the Law? It teaches us what is good and what is evil. Through the Tree of Good and Evil, God wanted to teach Adam "Obey God and you will live." God wanted to teach the same lesson to the Israelites and us by using the Law.

Second, "Knowledge" does not necessarily result in "putting into practice." Knowing a law does not guarantee that we will keep it. As a young parent I thought, "If I teach some rules and my child knows them, she will keep the rules." However, the reality was not always like that. The Pharisees in the Bible were smart and intelligent, knowing about Moses's Law and all the history and prophesies. They were experts! However, they did not see that they could not earn God's favor or build their righteousness by keeping the Law. Adam already "knew" that he and his wife should not eat the fruit from the Tree. However, his knowledge was not automatically connected to his obedience. In reality, the Law does not teach us what we are able to keep but instead leads us to realize how ungodly, helpless and sinful we are. Paul says that through the Law we come to know sin.

Third, The Tree of Knowledge of Good and Evil and the Law, both reveal what is inside the heart. The problem was not the Tree. The problem was the greed and pride in Adam's heart. The tree was just a tool that makes what is inside of Adam's heart float up to the surface. It was not the Law but the sin that "takes an opportunity through the Law, deceiving us and killing" (Romans 7:7-8). Keeping the Law and building self-righteousness is a tempting idea. Doesn't it sound more logical to "keep the Law and earn the ticket to Heaven?" Isn't this idea the whole foundation of most religions? Self-righteousness seems something to delight the eyes and desirable to make a person wise! Paul said, "Since they did not know the righteousness that comes from God and sought to establish their own, they did not submit to God's righteousness" (Romans 10:3).

Knowing Good and Evil does not save you, only the Tree of Life, Jesus, can save you! The Tree of Knowledge of Good and Evil and the Law are not a trap leading us to death. No, they are the GRACE of God! How can we realize that we need the Tree of Life without experiencing death from "the Tree of Knowledge of Good and Evil?" How can we come to know we need a Savior, without the experiences of hopelessness and condemnation we feel from the Law?

We all have our own standards about what is good and evil but do not have the abilities to put all the knowledge into practice. Our Lord is different. Isaiah 7:14-15 says "Therefore the Lord Himself will give you a sign: Behold, a virgin will be with child and bear a son, and she will call His name Immanuel. He will eat curds and honey at the time

He knows enough to *refuse* evil and *choose* good." Not only did our Lord Jesus know what was good and evil but he also chose good and refused evil. Jesus fulfilled every righteous standard of God when he was on the earth. Finally his death on the Cross was the pinnacle of satisfying God's requirements: Love and Justice. The death of Christ brought life for the people. Knowing what is good and evil cannot give us life. Only Jesus, the Tree of Life, gives life.

5 LIVING WATER

Now a river flowed out of Eden to water the garden;
and from there it divided and became four rivers.
(Genesis 2:10)

Now on the last day, the great day of the feast,
Jesus stood and cried out, saying,
"If anyone is thirsty, let him come to Me and drink.
"He who believes in Me, as the Scripture said,
'From his innermost being will flow rivers of living water.'"
But this He spoke of the Spirit, whom those who believed in Him were to
receive; for the Spirit was not yet given,
because Jesus was not yet glorified.
(John 7:37-39)

Then he showed me a river of the water of life, clear as crystal, coming
from the throne of God and of the Lamb, in the middle of its street.
On either side of the river was the tree of life,
bearing twelve kinds of fruit, yielding its fruit every month;
and the leaves of the tree were for the healing of the nations.
(Revelation 22:1-2)

What did the river in the Garden of Eden look like? What would the current sound like? I cannot begin to imagine how beautiful, crystal-clean and fresh it was. The river was watering the whole garden: all the plants, animals and Adam and Eve. The river was not only for the garden. It was not a pond or a lake. God called it a *river*, which flows out to other places. The Bible says the river was separated into four headwaters: the Pishon (meaning increase), the Gihon (bursting forth), the Hiddekel[1] (rapid), and the Euphrates (fruitfulness). Through these names I can feel the dynamic force, the power, and the energy that came from the water. I imagine that this water may have had healing power and may have rejuvenated the drinker. How great it would be to sip a little bit of that water for my thirsty throat and wash my dirty face and tired hands! But we lost access to that water when Adam broke his covenant with God.

Adam could not bequeath the living water to us, but God sent the last Adam, Jesus (1 Corinthians 15:45), to reopen the access to the living water. Jesus shouted "if anyone is thirsty, come to Me and drink." John 7:39 says that this water Jesus that spoke of is the Holy Spirit.

Revelation 22:1 describes a beautiful picture of this living water. John saw "a river of the water of life, clear as crystal, coming from the throne of God and of the Lamb." How powerful this water is! We see the Tree of life here again, bearing fruit every month, and even the leaves are herbal medicine. Yes! The Living Water comes from the throne of God and the Lamb, making His people alive to bear the fruit of the Spirit and to heal the nations with the Gospel.

---

[1] Genesis 2:14 (King James Version) The NIV uses Tigris.

The living water comes from the throne of God and the Lamb (Revelation 22:1). This verse sounds like a promise to me. If Jesus the Lamb is on the throne of my life, I taste and drink the life-giving water. This water cannot stagnate because it is a river! The Power of Life flows out to the world. Jesus makes His people branches of the Tree of Life, bearing fruit of the Spirit without ceasing. Jesus makes the leaves from the branches for healing their families, neighbors and the people in the remote places. The people filled with the Holy Spirit go out like the four rivers of Eden: Pishon (increase), Gihon (bursting forth), Hiddekel (rapid) and Euphrates (fruitfulness)!

6 THE LAMB

And he looked at Jesus as He walked, and said,
"Behold, the Lamb of God!" (John 1:36)

I do not speak Chinese but I know some Chinese letters since the Korean language has borrowed many words from Chinese. The Korean Hangul alphabet is based on sound like the Roman alphabet; however, Chinese characters are based mainly on images. So you can guess the meaning for some basic characters. Can you guess the three characters below?

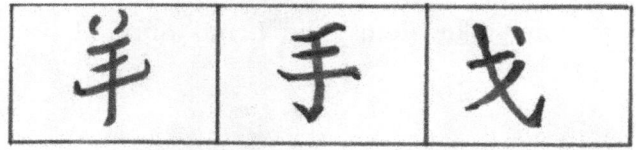

Here are some clues.

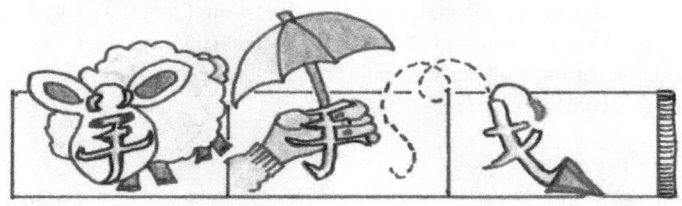

The first character means "lamb", the second one "hand" and the last one "lance or spear" First, what would be the meaning if hand and spear are combined? 我 This symbol means "Self, I, me" and if you add "lamb" on top, it makes 義. This symbol means "righteousness". It describes a sacrifice of a lamb that is killed with a spear, and then put the bleeding lamb upon "self". The Ancient Chinese somehow knew that men cannot be justified through their own efforts and deeds but needed a sacrifice.[2]

This truth is exactly what the Bible says: Jesus is our sacrificial Lamb. The only way we can be justified in the eyes of God is to cover ourselves with the blood of Jesus. The Bible says Jesus, who is completely God and completely man, became flesh and dwelled among the people, lived a life without sin, and finally gave himself away as a sacrifice to bring us back to God. Jesus the Lamb is the only sacrifice that can provide reconciliation. He is the Lamb who can justify you and me in the eyes of God. And not only you and me, but also all people: high and low, rich and poor, men and women, with no regard to skin color. Jesus, the Lamb of God, is our righteousness.

---

[2] I learned this interpretation from [Kang, C.H. and Nelson, Ethel R. (1979) The Discovery of Genesis: How the Truths of Genesis Were Found Hidden in the Chinese Language.] This book has more interesting findings about how some other Chinese letters correspond to elements of Genesis.

7 BONE OF MY BONES

The man said, "This is now bone of my bones, And flesh of my flesh."
(Genesis 2:23a)

I am the vine, you are the branches.
(John 15:5a)

Sometimes I have felt the worries of the world pressing down on me so badly, almost choking me.

Sometimes I have felt like a lonely kite whose string has been cut off from any connection.

Sometimes I have felt rejected and distant, even from someone who was supposedly close and friendly.

Sometimes I have been so upset, my head seemed on fire. If I were to pour several buckets of cold water on my head, steam would come out.

When I felt like that, the Words of God, "*I am the vine you are a branch*", saved me. To me this sounds like a New Testament version of Genesis 2:23 "bone of my bones and flesh of my flesh". If I am a branch of the Tree, I am part of *Him*. He regards me as His own body and He will take care of me as part of His body.

Jesus said, "Saul, Saul, why are you persecuting Me?" (Acts 9:4). But Saul did not persecute Jesus; he persecuted the disciples. Jesus did not say "Why are you persecuting my disciples?", because His people are part of His body.

Jesus takes my pain, my hurts and my suffering as His. What a sweet comfort His children have!

8 ADAM'S FAILURE AND JESUS' VICTORY

Then to Adam He said,
"Because you have listened to the voice of your wife,
and have eaten from the tree about which I commanded you, saying,
'You shall not eat from it';
Cursed is the ground because of you;
In toil you will eat of it All the days of your life.
(Genesis 3:17)

But He turned and said to Peter, "Get behind Me, Satan!
You are a stumbling block to Me;
for you are not setting your mind on God's interests, but man's."
(Matthew 16:23)

What words would hurt you the most? A curse from an enemy? a criticism from a rival? a slander from a jealous neighbor? When I read Genesis 3:17, I thought that the sweet words from a close friend can be poisonous, even if the words seem to give good advice. Our first Adam listened to Eve (who was tricked by the Serpent's lies), not God. Eve did not know what was really good for Adam. He should have obeyed God. Her suggestion and Adam's choice destroyed not only their lives in Eden but also their relationships and all their descendants including you and me. Sin and death came to the world and reigned through Adam's failure.

Jesus, however, did not fail like Adam. Jesus won in the very spot where Adam failed. Peter was one of Jesus' closest friends and disciples. Peter was destined to be a leader of the first Church, which is like the bride to Christ. Jesus loved Peter and Peter knew it. Peter did the same thing Eve did to Adam. He suggested an easier way and he was very certain it was a GOOD way for Jesus.

In that moment, I imagine that all the angels in the heaven must have had fallen silent, watching and listening to see how Jesus would react. This moment in Jesus' life was critical for the whole world. Perhaps the angels remembered the moment Adam failed and sin and death came into the world. Now, would a dramatic reversal happen to the human race? They did not need to wait so long to see the result!

Jesus answered, "Get behind Me, Satan! You are a stumbling block to Me; for you are not setting your mind on God's interests, but man's." Jesus passed the test! He did not fail! He won! I imagine clapping and cheerful sounds of shouting in heaven. At the moment Jesus refused Peter's desperate request, surely Peter's face must have tuned red. But that moment of embarrassment was much better for him than belonging eternally to Adam's failure.

I see Adam in me. How can I resist the sweet words of my close, reliable friends? Even Abram did not resist when Sarai gave him Hagar to solve their infertility. However, if Jesus lives and reigns in me he will give me strength and wisdom enough to refuse the sweet words. And he will let me set my mind on God's interest, not man's. And even though I cannot hear with my ears, the angels will also clap and shout for the victory when I submit my will to God.

9 TEMPTATION

And behold, a voice out of the heaven said,
"This is My beloved Son, in whom I am well-pleased",

Then Jesus was led up by the Spirit into the wilderness
to be tempted by the devil.
And after He had fasted forty days and forty nights,
He then became hungry.

And the tempter came and said to Him,
"If You are the Son of God, command that these stones become bread."
But He answered and said,
"It is written, 'Man shall not live on bread alone,
but on every word that proceeds out of the mouth of God.'"
(Matthew 3:17~4:4)

Before I read Genesis closely, I assumed Adam would not have had to work before he was fallen. In Eden, I thought Adam would play with Eve and the animals all day long, maybe hide-and-seek, and pick fruit and eat whenever he would want, and be loved by God and the angels.

I was wrong. Genesis 2:15 clearly says God put Adam into the garden to cultivate it and keep it. Before Adam sinned, he worked. God gave Adam two missions. One was to cultivate Eden and the other one was to keep Eden. Keep Eden from what? Was there any enemy threatening the garden? I thought Eden was supposed to be already well-protected by the strict security system provided by the Creator. But God gave Adam a responsibility to protect the beautiful garden from something. The very next verse gives me some clue as to how Adam could protect Eden and from whom. The Lord God said "From any tree of the garden you may eat freely; but from the tree of the knowledge of good and evil you shall not eat, for in the day that you eat from it you will surely die" (Genesis 2: 16-17). Notice the connection. In verse 16 God said "keep Eden", and then God gave Adam the commandment.

God is an omniscient God. God knew how Satan would attack Adam and Eve ahead. Satan did not attack them with sword or violence. Satan did not break the lock of the gate of Eden. Satan's weapon was questions and words that led Adam and Eve to doubt God's love. How could Adam keep Eden? The way was to trust God and keep His command.

Oh, Eden, this special place, was a place not to be kept with locks, security system, swords, guns or military maneuvers. This place was a place to be protected by God's children who would trust God's faithfulness and obey His commandments. God had already given Adam the way to keep Eden. The commandment was the key. If Adam could keep the commandment, he could protect not only Eden, but also his life and Eve's life. God had given Adam the clue in the form of a commandment before the temptation came to him.

Unfortunately, Adam and Eve did not trust God's word at the critical moment. They trusted the Serpent. Even though they had the key to protect Eden, it was no good. Here we can see, when God gives us commandments, it is because God loves us and wants us to be well and happy. God's commandments and laws are not meant to limit human freedom. His words are the key to protect an Eden-like life for us.

Adam failed to protect Eden from Satan because he did not trust God. Through one man, Adam, sin and death reigned over all of the human race. But, here is the good news. Thousands of years after Adam, another man succeeded in protecting the world from Satan by trusting God's words. Matthew 4 tells us this story. Satan came and used (craftily) the words of God to tempt Jesus. God the Father already said, "This is My beloved Son, in whom I am well-pleased" (Matthew 3:17). Since God said so, it is the truth. No one needs to prove God's truth. But Satan asked Jesus to prove it by turning stones to bread. Jesus was not at all ensnared by Satan's trick. Jesus did not need to prove that he was the son of God. Jesus did not use visible weapons to fight against Satan. His weapons were the words of God, the double-edged sharp swords. Our last Adam protected the world through obeying the word of God. He has reopened the Garden of Eden for those who trust and love him.

10 THE LADDER

"Come, let Us go down and there confuse their language,
so that they will not understand one another's speech."
So the LORD scattered them abroad from there
over the face of the whole earth; and they stopped building the city.
Therefore its name was called Babel,
because there the LORD confused the language of the whole earth;
and from there the LORD scattered them abroad
over the face of the whole earth.
(Genesis 11:7-9)

He had a dream, and behold, a ladder was set on the earth
with its top reaching to heaven; and behold,
the angels of God were ascending and descending on it.
(Genesis 28:12)

And He said to him, "Truly, truly, I say to you,
you will see the heavens opened
and the angels of God ascending and descending on the Son of Man."
(John 1:51)

Since I came to the U.S. at age 26, I know how hard it is to learn a foreign language! I thought "if the human race had only one common and universal language, I would not be suffering from trying to learn English!" Why do we have all these different languages that make it so hard to talk to each other? Even within the same language people often say, "It is hard for parents to understand their teenagers", or "Men are from Mars and Women are from Venus: They need interpreters!" or "Older generations need to learn the new languages of the younger generations." How did all of the differences among languages, genders and generations get started? Genesis 11 tells us.

A long time ago, the whole earth used the same language. The same language was a big blessing for the ancient people but they used it against the will of God. God's plan was for the people to spread and multiply on the earth; and God also promised He would NOT destroy all the creatures on the earth by another flood (Genesis 9). However it seems that the next generation after Noah's Flood did not trust God. The people started building an extraordinarily high tower. They had two purposes: They wanted to be famous and they did not want to be scattered on the face of the earth. They did not accept "being scattered" as a blessing. Perhaps they thought a tall tower would be a safe place from a scary flood they had heard about from their forefathers. They suppressed the truth about why God had to judge the whole world and what God promised afterward.

They had their own version of "advanced" technology. Genesis 11:3 says they had "brick" for stone and "bitumen" for mortar. Bitumen is like tar, a sticky glue for the bricks. This verse tells us they had a more advanced technology than in the past. Today, supercomputers and the internet are some of our technologies, and we also have made many scientific advances. Some people say our science has invaded God's territory. The ancient people in Genesis 11 may have thought the same way: "By building a high tower with brick and bitumen we can invade God's Territory: Heaven."

To prevent the people from building the tower, the first thing God did was "to come down" to investigate the situation. His coming down did not take place often in the Old Testament. He came down to investigate Sodom in the time of Abraham (Genesis 18:21). And in the book of Exodus God came down to rescue His people from the Egyptians' oppression (Exodus 3:8). Why did God "come down"? He is the eternal all-knowing God. He has no need to come down to learn anything. But He came down in these cases to let us know how important the situations were to Him.

Next, God confused their language so they would not understand each other. Genesis 11:6 tells us that the people could begin this work because they had the same language. After God confused their language, the people stopped building the tower, which was called "Babel". They could not have completed it anyway, even without interference from God. Who can make a tower that can reach up to heaven?

God could have used many means to punish the builders of Babel. Why did God choose "confusion of the language"? Our gracious God was opening a way to bless them in the midst of their rebellious acts. "Spreading over the face of the earth" was a blessed plan of God from the start (Genesis 1:28 & 9:7), and God Himself fulfilled this purpose.

A thousand years later, God chose one man among the scattered people. His name was Abraham. God also chose the man's grandchild Jacob to show us God's own plan, His idea about connecting heaven and earth. The tower was a human effort to connect earth to heaven. But God's plan was to send down a ladder from heaven to earth. God gave Jacob a dream that showed him a ladder resting on the earth, with its top reaching to heaven, and the angels of God were ascending and descending on it (Genesis 28:12). Jacob also saw the Lord standing above the ladder, telling of his plan to bless all the people on the earth: "Your children will be like the dust of the earth, they will spread out all over the earth; and in your children all the people of the earth will be blessed" (Genesis 28:14).

As God promised, one of Jacob's descendants has become the source of blessing for all the people of the earth. The ladder that Jacob saw in his dream was not a structure; it was a person. Jesus described himself as the ladder saying "Truly, truly, I say to you, you will see the heavens opened and the angels of God ascending and descending on the Son of Man. (John 1:51)" Jesus, who came from heaven, has become the connection between heaven and earth through His sacrifice on the cross. The tower of Babel, all human efforts and advanced technologies cannot reach heaven. But God gave us the solution. Jesus is the only way to the Father. (John 14:6, *"Jesus said to him, 'I am the way, and the truth, and the life; no one comes to the Father but through Me.'"*)

When Jesus is our connection to the Father, walls of separation collapse between people (John 17:22 and Ephesians 2:14). In Acts 2 Jesus' disciples spoke foreign languages that they had never learned before, declaring "the mighty deeds of God" (2:11). The foreign people who visited Jerusalem were surprised, saying "And how is it that we each hear them in our own language to which we were born? (2:8)"

The occurrence in Acts 2 was temporary but I believe in heaven there will be no more language barriers. We will be able to speak with Abraham or Jacob without an interpreter. We'll have no more burden of learning English or other foreign languages because we won't be living in a foreign land anymore!

11 THE SEED

*In your seed all the nations of the earth shall be blessed,
because you have obeyed My voice.*
(Genesis 22: 18)

*Now the promises were spoken to Abraham
and to his seed. He does not say, 'And to seeds,' as referring to many,
but rather to one, 'And to your seed,'
that is, Christ.*
(Galatians 3:16)

Much of the Old Testament chronicles the history of Israel and God's interaction with the patriarchs before Israel became a nation. However, both of the Old and New Testament verses at the beginning of this chapter confirm that God's intention in selecting Abraham was to bless all mankind. God chose Abraham not only to give him a son, a land, and many descendants, but also eventually to bless "all" through Christ.

After Adam and Eve disobeyed God by trusting Satan's word rather than God's word, they suffered the consequences of their sin: death. But God the Father gave them a promise. "Her seed shall bruise you [Satan] on the head, and you [Satan] shall bruise him on the heel"(Genesis 3:15). Many Bible scholars believe that this verse is a prophecy about Jesus's death on the cross and also His victory over Satan.

God used the word "seed" to describe the coming messiah. Many years after Adam, God chose Abraham and put the Seed in Abraham's family line. He was like a pot that contained the Seed. Since the Seed was important, God cared for Abraham and his family in a special way. God blessed, protected, and made an everlasting covenant with him.

So, what is a seed? It is part of a plant. If you put it into the ground, it grows into a plant. (1) Seeds are usually small. (2) They have life. Life makes them grow and multiply. (3) Seeds also mean the starting or the beginning. For example, if you say "I need seed money", you mean that you need money to start a business or some other endeavor. (4) Seeds are valuable. If you are a potato farmer, you do not eat the "seed potatoes". You keep them for the next planting. (5) Seeds are for teaching us about faith. We cannot see a big tree in this little seed. You cannot see a forest of countless trees in a little seed, with your physical eyes, but you can see it with the eyes of faith.

God taught Abraham about faith in the coming Messiah by using the word seed. "I will greatly multiply your seed as the stars of the heavens; and your seed shall possess the gate of their enemies; and in your seed all the nations of the earth shall be blessed." (Genesis 22:17-18) I believe that these verses were God's promise to send the Messiah through Abraham's family line and that the Messiah would bless the whole world. Only this Messiah can break the curse that our sins brought on us and make the blessings of God flow into the whole world again.

About 2,000 years after Abraham, Jesus was born as Abraham's descendant. Finally Messiah had come as God promised. Jesus said to the Jews, "Your father Abraham rejoiced to see My day, and he saw it and was glad" (John 8:57). Abraham put his faith in the coming Messiah, and God credited the faith as righteousness to Abraham. The same thing is true today. If you put your faith in the Messiah who came and is coming again, God has promised he will take your faith in Jesus Christ as your righteousness.

Jesus became a curse for us on the cross (Galatians 3:13). He took all the curses that belonged to us and replaced the curse with the blessing of God. Jesus is the Seed of blessing. If the Seed is planted in you, the soil, the seed will grow and bear the fruit of eternal life. With the eyes of faith, we can see the Kingdom of God in the Seed. Someday, we will see the fulfillment of the Kingdom of God. Do you have the Seed?

42

12 ANOINTED KING

Then after his[Abraham's] return
from the defeat of Chedorlaomer
and the kings who were with him,
the king of Sodom went out to meet him
at the valley of Shaveh(that is, the King's Valley).

And Melchizedek king of Salem brought out bread and wine;
now he was a priest of God Most High.
And He blessed him and said,

"Blessed be Abram of God Most High, possessor of heaven and earth;
And blessed be God Most High,
Who has delivered your enemies into your hand."
And He gave him a tenth of all.
(Genesis 14:17~20)

The LORD has sworn and will not change His mind,
"You are a priest forever
according to the order of Melchizedek."
The Lord is at Your right hand;
He will shatter kings in the day of His wrath.
He will judge among the nations…
(Psalms 110:4~6a)

The word Christ or Messiah means "the anointed one". "Anoint" means to pour oil on a part of the body. In the Old Testament, only three positions of authority were anointed by God: prophet, priest and king. Jesus, the Christ, is all three. Believing in Christ is not merely believing in God. It is believing in Jesus as the only One anointed by God as Prophet, Priest, and King.

In Genesis 14, Abraham foreshadows the kingship of Christ. At that time, there was a war in Canaan. Five kings were battling against four other kings. Abraham remained neutral in this war until one side captured the family and possessions of his nephew Lot. his nephew Lot's family and all his possessions. He then joined the battle to save Lot. Genesis 14:14-16 tells us that Abraham then joined the battle, defeated the kings and saved Lot. Verse 17 says that after Abraham returned from his victory, he met Melchizedek, King of Salem. This king had not been a part of this war. His name tells who he was: he was a king of righteousness and a king of peace (Hebrews 7:2).

Melchizedek was a unique king because he was also a priest. In the Old Testament time, there were two types of priesthood. One, the order of Aaron (the Levitical priesthood), was established by the Mosaic Law after the Exodus. The other type, the order of Mechizedek, was set up by God's oath (Hebrews 7:21 and Psalm 110:4), not by the Law. God never allowed a Levitical priest to be a king. Psalm 110:4 says God the Father has appointed Jesus Christ as the everlasting Priest in *the order of Melchizedek*. And then look at the next verses. What will this unique *Priest* do? He will act as King. He will crush kings on the day of His wrath and judge the nations.

God shows us a picture of the coming Christ. Abraham defeated the Canaanite kings and rescued Lot and his family. It is a king's task.

Next, we see Melchizedek, who brought out bread and wine to bless Abraham, and then Abraham gave his tithe to him. It is a priest's task. From Abraham's victory in Genesis, through Melchizedek's unique kingship in Psalms, through the resemblance between Christ and Mechizedek in Hebrews and finally Christ's triumph in the Book of Revelation, we see the theme of the anointed one grow into the fullness of Christ. When Jesus returns he will rule with an iron scepter!

13 ANOINTED PROPHET

Now therefore, restore the man's wife, for he is a prophet,
and he will pray for you and you will live.
But if you do not restore her, know that you shall surely die,
you and all who are yours.
(Genesis 20:7)

Some of the people therefore, when they heard these words,
were saying, "This certainly is the Prophet."
(John 7:40)

and that He may send Jesus, the Christ appointed for you,
whom heaven must receive until the period of restoration
of all things about which God spoke by the mouth
of His holy prophets from ancient time.

Moses said, 'The Lord God will raise up for you a prophet like me from
your brethren, to him you shall give heed to everything He says to you.
And it will be that every soul that does not heed that prophet shall be
utterly destroyed from among the people"
(Acts 3:20-23)

In Genesis 20, Abraham moved south and stayed in Gerar, where he met Abimelech, king of the region. Abraham was afraid of the pagan king. He said "Because I thought, surely there is no fear of God in this place, and they will kill me because of my wife (20:11)." Out of fear, Abraham asked Sarah, his wife, to tell the king a half-truth: 'I am the sister of Abraham'. She was a half-sister of her husband, but she did not say that she was also his wife. Thinking Sarah was not married, Abimelech took her into his house.

That night God warned Abimelech in his dream to send Sarah back to Abraham safely, saying "if you do not restore her, know that you shall surely die and you and all who are yours" (v.7). God called Abraham "a prophet" in Abimelech's dream, and then God added that the prophet would pray for Abimelech and that he would live (v.7).

To Abimelech, although Abraham had many possessions and people, he was a nomad and subject to Abimelech's rule. This pagan king believed that he had nothing to fear from Abraham. But God Himself made Abimelech fearful of Abraham. The next morning after the dream, Abimelech called all his servants and told them what God had said to him and they were frightened. Abimelech not only sent Sarah back to Abraham with a thousand pieces of silver for her vindication, but also he gave sheep, oxen, and servants to Abraham. Moreover, Abimelech allowed Abraham to choose wherever Abraham wanted to live. After all these things happened, Abraham prayed to God for Abimelech. Verse 17 says "Abraham prayed to God, and God healed Abimelech and his wife and his maids, so they bore children." Perhaps through this experience, Abraham discovered how much God cared for him and what a privilege he had in prayer.

About four hundred years later, God, through Moses, gave the Israelites a warning similar to the one God had given Abimelech. He told people, "The LORD your God will raise up for you a prophet like me from among you, from your fellow Israelites, you shall *listen to him*...I [God] will put My words in his mouth. He will tell them everything I command him" (Deuteronomy 18:15, 18b, NIV).

This Prophet that Moses spoke of came to the earth around 1,500 years after Moses' time. The people of Israel were supposed to listen to everything the Prophet said to them. What if they did not listen and obey the Prophet? God says "and it will be that every soul that does not heed that prophet shall be utterly destroyed from among the people" (Acts 3:23). In the New Testament, Peter proclaims that the Prophet is Jesus (Acts 3:20). Peter learned that Jesus is the Anointed Prophet not only from Moses's Deuteronomy, but he also heard what God the Father said when Jesus was transfigured on a high mountain. Mark 9:7 says, "Then a cloud formed, overshadowing them, and a voice came out of the cloud, 'This is My beloved Son, *listen to Him.*'"

Listen to Him! I want to inscribe those three words on my heart. Before I met Jesus, I was like Abimelech, who did not believe. I tried to be king of my own life and took whatever I wanted if I could. After Jesus came and found me, I gradually discovered that He is the one I should subject myself to. When He prays for me I can live. If I do not listen to Him, I shall surely die.

14 ANOINTED PRIEST

> Then he [Abraham] said, "Oh may the Lord not be angry,
> and I shall speak only this once;
> suppose ten are found there?" And He said,
> "I will not destroy it on account of the ten."
> (Genesis 18:32)
>
> Therefore, since we have a great high priest
> who has passed through the heavens, Jesus the Son of God,
> let us hold fast our confession.
> For we do not have a high priest
> who cannot sympathize with our weaknesses,
> but One who has been tempted in all things
> as we are, yet without sin.
> (Hebrews 4:14-15)

Jesus is Christ, the Anointed One! This good news is what Paul and the other apostles proclaimed until their deaths. The aspects of Christ as King, Prophet, and Priest can be found in Abraham. So far I have shared the aspects of King and Prophet. Now, let's look at how God shows us the "priest" in Abraham. What is a priest? A priest stands between God and man; and can be called a 'mediator' (1Timothy 2:5). A priest prays on behalf of people before God. This special job was not something anyone who wants to do it can do. God Himself chose people to carry out this task.

Before God destroyed Sodom and Gomorrah, He told Abraham what He was going to do. In Genesis 18:17, God told his angels "Shall I hide from Abraham what I am about to do?" When God told Abraham His plan, Abraham was concerned for his nephew Lot, and so he stood between God and Lot as a priest would between God and the Israelites in later days.

Abraham asked God if He would spare Sodom and Gomorrah for the sake of any righteous people, finally as few as ten, who lived there. God said he would spare the cities for ten righteous people, but only righteous Lot and his family could be found. Genesis 19:29a says "Thus it came about when God destroyed the cities of the valley, *that God remembered Abraham*, and sent Lot out of the midst of the overthrow."

This story shows us that Jesus will save the believers of all the nations on the last Judgment Day. Romans 5:9b says, "we shall be saved from the wrath of God through Him [Jesus]." When God pours out His wrath because of all the sinful acts of the world, He will remember what our Great High Priest, Jesus, did for us on the cross, and He will save the believers out of the midst of the overthrow!

15 SARAH AND MARY

Is anything too difficult for the LORD? At the appointed time
I will return to you, at this time next year, and Sarah will have a son
(Genesis 18:14)

The angel answered and said to her [Mary],
"The Holy Spirit will come upon you,
and the power of the Most High will overshadow you;
and for that reason the holy Child shall be called the Son of God.
And behold, even your relative Elizabeth has also conceived a son
in her old age; and she who was called barren is now in her sixth month.
"For nothing will be impossible with God."
(Luke 1:35-37)

Abraham and Sarah were too old to be able to have babies. In terms of having children, their bodies were as good as dead. The Bible says "Abraham was about hundred years old and Sarah's womb was also dead" (Romans 4:19). Then one day an angel of God told Abraham, "Sarah will have a baby boy next year", and when Sarah heard it, she laughed. "What? I am so old!" The angel asked Abraham "why did Sarah laugh? **Is anything too difficult for the Lord?**"

Two thousand years later, an angel said almost same thing to a girl, a many times great granddaughter of Sarah: "**Nothing is impossible with God.**" This time the girl was not old, but she was young and not married. Her name was Mary. She did not laugh but she was astonished, asking, "How can I have a baby?"

Before I became a Christian, I thought, "What, a virgin had a baby? God became a little human baby? This story is more ridiculous than fairy tales. Peter Pan and Cinderella make more sense." This story seemed ridiculous to me, not because the story is bad, but because the story is too good, too good to be true. If there is a God, the Creator, and Almighty God, did he become a human and live among us? It is too good to be true, isn't it? A great painter like Picasso could not enter his own drawing and be part of it, but God entered into the world he created. I was not able to believe it, not because the story was bad, but because the story was too good to be true.

I came to church one day and started to read the Bible. Through the Bible, I found I was spiritually dead. Like dead bodies, I had no feeling, no interest, no knowledge about God. By human standards, I was not so bad. I had never killed anyone or broken human laws, so by human standards I was not a criminal. But the Bible says "Anyone who hates his brother is a murderer" (1John 3:15). If you are angry with your brother, or say 'You fool', you will be in the fire of hell" (Matthew 5). I found God's standard to be much higher than I thought. If I hated someone, to God it was as if I had killed someone. By God's standard, I was 100% sinner. But, I also found that God promised that whoever believes in Jesus receives the gift of eternal life.

Just like Sarah and Mary I asked the same question, "How can I have this gift from God?" The same answer came to me: "**Nothing is impossible with God.**" Since Jesus came into my heart, I have found a new life. The old life becomes less and this new life becomes greater. The day I believed in Jesus was like my Christmas because I received the gift of a new life.

16 ISAAC

Abraham took the wood of the burnt offering
and laid it on Isaac his son,
and he took in his hand the fire and the knife.
So the two of them walked on together.
Isaac spoke to Abraham his father and said, "My father!"
And he said, "Here I am, my son."
And he said, "Behold, the fire and the wood,
but where is the lamb for the burnt offering?"

Abraham said, "God will provide for Himself the lamb
for the burnt offering, my son."
So the two of them walked on together.
Then they came to the place of which God had told him; and Abraham
built the altar there and arranged the wood,
and bound his son Isaac and laid him on the altar, on top of the wood.
Abraham stretched out his hand and took the knife to slay his son.
But the angel of the LORD called to him from heaven
and said, "Abraham, Abraham!"
And he said, "Here I am."

He said, "Do not stretch out your hand against the lad,
and do nothing to him; for now I know that you fear God,
since you have not withheld your son, your only son, from Me."
Then Abraham raised his eyes and looked, and behold,
behind him a ram caught in the thicket by his horns;

> and Abraham went and took the ram and offered him up
> for a burnt offering in the place of his son.
>
> Abraham called the name of that place
> The LORD Will Provide, as it is said to this day,
> "In the mount of the LORD it will be provided."
>
> (Genesis 22:6-14)

When Abraham was seventy five years old, God promised to give him many children and many descendants – as many as the stars he could see. At that time Abraham had no children at all. However, he believed God. He had faith in God's promise. God was pleased and credited Abraham's faith as righteousness because he believed God when the situation appeared hopeless. Twenty five years after God's promise, when Abraham and Sarah had completely lost their child bearing ability, God gave them Isaac. God could have given them a child while they were still in their child-bearing years but He did not. Why? It may be because God wanted to teach them Who He was: the giver of life. He can give life at any time, according to His will.

One day God called Abraham to test his faith. This time, God told Abraham to give his son Isaac as a burnt offering. God said "Take your son, your only son Isaac, whom you love, and go to a mountain I will show you." Isaac was carrying wood on his back and Abraham was holding a knife and fire. They had walked three days and arrived at the place God told him about, a mountain in the region of Moriah. Isaac was a teenager at the time. If he had wanted, he could have run away. But Isaac did not. He obeyed his father, whom he trusted. He lied down and closed his eyes.

If I were Abraham, my heart would be burning during the three day journey. It would be not easy for me to hold on to my faith. I would struggle to believe God is good and He had been good to me. It would be like a battle in my soul. The Bible does not describe what struggles Abraham went through in his heart during this test. Instead, it tells us that Abraham had faith in the promise of God because *"through Isaac"* God would send The Savior of all the people. God did not lie to Abraham. God always keeps his promise. God had been teaching Abraham this lesson for the last forty years. Even though Isaac would be dead, God could give life back to him because He is the God of life. With complete faith in God, Abraham took the knife and held it over his son, whom He loved more than his own life. At that moment, the angel of God shouted from heaven. "Abraham! Abraham! STOP! Don't do anything to your son…Now I know you fear God." Then God showed Abraham a lamb to use as a substitute, a replacement for Isaac's life.

Two thousand years later, a many times great grandson of Isaac was also carrying wood; a heavy wooden cross. This time the wood was for a burnt offering as well, but in a different way from Isaac's. This Son went up to the same mountainous area in the region of Mount Moriah, which had become Jerusalem and its vicinity by the time of Jesus. This time the Angel of God did not say "STOP." This Son, the Savior that God promised to Abraham, died. There was no substitute for Him because the Savior was the Lamb of God. This Son died. Genesis 22 foreshadows what God the Father would do for us two thousand years after Abraham. God the Father took His Son, His only begotten Son, whom He loves, Jesus, and sent him to a hill called Calvary, and offered Jesus there as an offering for my sin, for your sin.

God, like a movie director, delivered his important salvation message through dramatization. I see God, the director of life, communicating His salvation through real people and real life events. Genesis 22 is a beautiful drama but Abraham and Isaac were not actors. The way God communicates with us is sometimes beyond our imagination and intelligence. God *could have told* Abraham just plainly "two thousand years from now, the Seed from your family line, who is my only beloved, begotten Son, will go to a hill in the Land of Moriah, and offer himself as the sacrificial lamb to give you and your descendants eternal life." God did not choose this way. He actually put Abraham into His shoes and put Isaac into His Son's shoes so that down through the ages, people would remember this story and see Jesus as their substitute sacrifice.

17 ISAAC VS. ISHMAEL

Now Sarah saw the son of Hagar the Egyptian,
whom she had borne to Abraham, mocking.
Therefore she said to Abraham, "Drive out this maid and her son,
for the son of this maid shall not be an heir with my son Isaac."
The matter distressed Abraham greatly because of his son.
But God said to Abraham,
"Do not be distressed because of the lad and your maid; whatever Sarah
tells you, listen to her, for through Isaac your descendants shall be named.
(Genesis 21:9~12)

But as many as received Him, to them He gave the right to become children
of God, even to those who believe in His name, who were born,
not of blood nor of the will of the flesh nor of the will of man, but of God
(John 1:12~13)

And you brethren, like Isaac, are children of promise.
But as at that time he who was born according to the flesh persecuted him
who was born according to the Spirit, so it is now also. But what does the
Scripture say? "CAST OUT THE BONDWOMAN AND HER SON,
FOR THE SON OF THE BONDWOMAN SHALL NOT BE AN HEIR
WITH THE SON OF THE FREE WOMAN
(Galatians 4:28 ~30)

Sarai (her name means noble woman) had waited and waited for at least ten years for God to start giving her children, the descendants He had promised (Genesis 16:3). She had become anxious and made a hasty and wrong decision. She took her Egyptian maid Hagar and gave her to her husband. Abram (his name means high father) agreed, and between Abram and Hagar, Ishmael was born. Abram and Sarai did not know what consequences their action would bring in the future to themselves, to their children and to the history of Israel and human race.

But God was merciful. Despite the impatient action of Sarai and Abram, about a dozen years later God changed their names to Abraham (father of a multitude) and Sarah (princess), and gave them Isaac, the son of promise, born by the power of the Holy Spirit (Galatians 4:29). Sarah, a free woman, became a symbol of the New Covenant (Heavenly Jerusalem) whereas Hagar, a slave girl, became a symbol of the covenant of Law (Earthly Jerusalem) (Galatians 4:24-31).

Ishmael, as a thirteen year old boy, was physically stronger than one year old Isaac. Ishmael mocked (Genesis 21:9) and persecuted Isaac (Galatians 4:29). When Sarah discovered what Ishmael was doing, she told Abraham to drive out Hagar and Ishmael. Although Abraham was distressed, he listened to God's voice and made a decision in faith. He sent out Hagar and Ismael forever from his household.

I believe that Isaac and Ishmael represent two contrasting natures in most believers: spirit vs. flesh. In other words, Isaac is like the new self that wants to walk in newness of life through unity with Christ's death and resurrection (Romans 6:4). This nature seeks God's righteousness by faith and pursues life and peace. In contrast, Ishmael is like an old self. This nature seeks God's righteousness by works. This old self leads us to think we can satisfy God's standards with our own efforts, what Scripture calls acting in the "flesh". Romans 8:6-8 says, "For the mind set on the flesh is death, but the mind set on the Spirit is life and peace, because the mind set on the flesh is hostile toward God; for it does not subject itself to the law of God, for it is not even able to do so, and those who are in the flesh cannot please God."

The battle between Ishmael and Isaac occurs inside of me. There was a certain time in my life when I tried to please God with my own works. Ishmael inside of me wanted to have a good reputation and build up self-righteousness. I thought I knew what was the best for me and my family. My decisions were better than those of my husband or other people, and even God. I was not able to be patient with God's timing. These works I did on my own turned out in vain. I did not know that the works of my old nature could not please God. But God was gracious to me because of Jesus, just as He was to Sarah. Genesis 21:10 became God's voice to me: Drive out your "Ishmael"; keep only "Isaac."

18 EARLY IN THE MORNIG

So Abraham rose *early in the morning* and took bread and a skin of water and gave them to Hagar, putting them on her shoulder, and gave her the boy, and sent her away. And she departed and wandered about in the wilderness of Beersheba (Genesis 21:14)

Now Abraham arose *early in the morning* and went to the place where he had stood before the LORD
(Genesis 19:27)

So Abraham rose *early in the morning* and saddled his donkey, and took two of his young men with him and Isaac his son; and he split wood for the burnt offering, and arose and went to the place of which God had told him.
(Genesis 22:3)

In *the early morning*, while it was still dark, Jesus got up, left the house, and went away to a secluded place, and was praying there
(Mark 1:35)

Abraham was a man of obedience. When God commanded him to do something, Abraham carried it out first thing in the morning. We see this pattern throughout his life. What God was asking of Abraham was difficult in Genesis 21. Abraham had to send away his son Ishmael. Gen 21:11 says, "the matter distressed Abraham greatly because it concerned his son." However, when God said so, he stopped thinking and worrying. The very next morning Abraham simply obeyed. He also obeyed early in the morning when God told him to sacrifice his son Isaac.

This expression of obedience is found in Our Lord Jesus. When He was on the earth, He also got up early in the morning. He went to a quiet place to pray and listen to the Father. Our Lord modeled for us how to accomplish the will of God the Father, not His own. I pray the Lord molds the same pattern within me: to get up early in the morning to pray and to do the will of the Father.

19 CALL ON THE NAME OF THE LORD

To Seth, to him also a son was born; and he called his name Enosh
Then men began to call upon the name of the LORD
(Genesis 4:26)

Abraham planted a tamarisk tree at Beersheba, and there he called on the
name of the LORD, the Everlasting God.
(Genesis 21:33)

And it shall be that everyone who calls on the name of the Lord
will be saved.' "Men of Israel, listen to these words:
Jesus the Nazarene, a man attested to you
by God with miracles and wonders and signs
which God performed through Him in your midst,
just as you yourselves know
(Acts 2:21-22)

One day Abimelech, a pagan king of the region, came and asked Abraham to make a peace contract because God had shown that Abraham was special in the sight of God. Genesis 21:21-22 says, "[Abimelech] spoke to Abraham, saying, *"God is with you in all that you do; therefore, swear to me here by God that you will not falsely with me or with my offspring or with my posterity, but according to the kindness that I have shown to you, you shall show to me and to the land in which you have sojourned."*

I imagined the feeling of relief Abraham that would have with this contract. Now he, his children and grandchildren could stay safely in this foreign land. Since I am an immigrant, a green card holder in the United States, I do not take my right to stay in this land for granted. I know the relief when a foreigner receives permission to stay permanently, to have protection for possessions and legal status in a new land. Genesis 21 tells us how God resolved three major important issues in Abraham's life: Isaac was born, Ismael was sent out, and Abraham got his green card! These issues were resolved before God tested Abraham in Genesis 22, the climax of his journey toward God.

Right after Abraham completed the contract with Abimelech, he planted a tamarisk tree, but not because he needed another tree. Verse 33 says he called on the name of the Lord, the Everlasting God. It was not the first time. He called the name of the Lord to the east of Bethel and built an altar in the early years (Genesis 12: 8, 13:4). The words "call on the name of the LORD" are first found in Genesis 4:26, where after Enosh, a grandson of Adam, was born, people began to call on the name of the LORD. This practice was continued by Abraham.

"Calling on" in this context is not just saying God's name to get His attention. "Calling upon" implies worship, because Abraham either built an altar or planted a tree to remember what God had done for him or who God was to him. This phrase is also found in Joel 2:32. God promised that "everyone who calls on the name of the Lord will be saved," and this verse is quoted by Peter (Acts 2:21) and Paul (Romans 10:13) in the New Testament. The name of the Lord is Jesus. My altar, my tamarisk tree is the Cross of Jesus. I worship my God there, calling on the name of the Lord Jesus.

The Old Rugged Cross
by George Bennard (1873 - 1958)

In that old rugged cross,
stained with blood so divine,
A wondrous beauty I see,
For 'twas on that old cross Jesus suffered and died,
To pardon and sanctify me.
So I'll cherish the old rugged cross,
Till my trophies at last I lay down;
I will cling to the old rugged cross,
And exchange it someday for a crown.

20 HERE I AM

Abraham : Now it came about after these things, that God tested Abraham, and said to him, "Abraham!" And he said, **"Here I am."** (Genesis 22:1)

Samuel: ...that the LORD called Samuel; and he said, **"Here I am."** (I Samuel 3:4)

Isaiah : Then I heard the voice of the Lord saying, "Whom shall I send? And who will go for us?" And I said, "**Here am I**. Send me!" (Isaiah 6:8)

Peter and Andrew: And He [Jesus] said to them, "Follow Me, and I will make you fishers of men." **Immediately** they left their nets and followed Him (Matthew 4:19-20)

Ananias: Now there was a disciple at Damascus named Ananias; and the Lord said to him in a vision, "Ananias." And he said, "**Here I am**, Lord." (Acts 9:10).

God is a God we can call upon. He is also a God who calls the names of people. God and His people call each other. Through the ages, people have responded in various ways to God's calling. Adam hid. Cain lied and even got angry enough to kill. Still others who loved God responded by saying, "Here I am."

Abraham, in Genesis 22 said "Here I am" three times. The first "Here I am" is in verse 1: God called his name one time: "Abraham". This calling was to invite Abraham into a message, demonstrating what God the Father would do with His only begotten Son two thousand years later. In the first call, Abraham walked in obedience to God's command to sacrifice his only son.

The second "Here I am" is the answer to Isaac's calling in the middle of his journey in verse 7: *"My father"* "Here I am, my son" *"Behold, the fire and the wood, but where is the lamb for the burnt offering?"* If I had been Abraham, I might have wondered how I would respond. How could I control all of my doubt, confusion, fear and pain? When Isaac called his name, Abraham plainly and calmly said, "Here I am."

The question *"where is the lamb for the burnt offering?"* made me think of the prayer of Jesus at Gethsemane the night before He became our sacrifice on the cross (Matthew 26:39). God the Son, called His Father. *"My Father"* Jesus, however, did *not* ask the question because He already knew what would happen.

God called Abraham again at the very moment when he was about to slay his son. God called his name twice: "Abraham Abraham." In the Bible when a name is called twice, it seems to signify either an urgency, an exclamation, or a way to calm down a person in action, for example, "Lord, Lord" (Matthew 25:11, Matthew 7:22) or "Martha, Martha" (Luke 10:41). At this calling from

God, Abraham had proven his heart, his ear, and his muscles were all tuned to hearing God's voice. He stopped right away and said "Here I am." God then poured out all the blessing, revealing more about the Seed (verses 17, 18). I can hear God's voice of excitement and satisfaction just as a father cheered his beloved son, who had just led the biggest victory. Abraham was the forefather of "Here I am" of all the following believers: Samuel, Isaiah, Peter, and Ananias.

Lord,

I know how strong my old sinful nature is,
which wants to hide from You as did Adam;
and avoid responsibility for brothers and sisters, as did Cain.

But I, also, know that by the power of the Holy Spirit
You can lead me to conquer my old sinful nature,
and to say "Here I am",
as did Abraham and carry out your will,
as did your followers.

21 BROAD PATH OR NARROW PATH

So Abram went forth as the LORD had spoken to him;
and Lot went with him (Genesis 12:4a)

So Abram said to Lot, "Please let there be no strife between you and me, nor between my herdsmen and your herdsmen, for we are brothers. "Is not the whole land before you? Please separate from me; if to the left, then I will go to the right; or if to the right, then I will go to the left." Lot lifted up his eyes and saw all the valley of the Jordan, that it was well watered everywhere--this was before the LORD destroyed Sodom and Gomorrah--like the garden of the LORD,
like the land of Egypt as you go to Zoar.
(Genesis 13:8-10)

If you read a Korean Bible, Genesis 12:4a sounds like this: Abram followed the Lord's word while Lot followed Abram. These words show an interesting contrast. One man followed God, but the other man followed a man. They were together for a while, but then the time came when they had to separate. They chose opposite directions. Abraham remained in the wilderness and Lot selected the fertile land with advanced cities.

Who was wiser? Lot and his family and workers may have thought their choice was more reasonable. Advanced cities in a fertile land would provide what Lot thought that he and his family needed. However, life in Sodom and Gomorrah was tough. The whole family had become captives during a war (Genesis 14) and were fortunate that Abram rescued them. But they still preferred to stay in the land after the war. Eventually they experienced the total destruction of their hometown (Genesis 18). Who should Lot have been trusting all along? God, who would provide even in the wilderness. Lot ended up in a cave. He survived but his descendants would one day make trouble for Israel. In contrast, Abraham not only kept all his material blessings, but also had descendants as numerous as the stars in the sky. Abraham chose a narrow path while Lot chose a broad one (Matthew 7:13).

Was Lot a righteous man? Yes. Peter says so, and he also tells us the kind of life that Lot lived: "and if he rescued Lot, a righteous man, who was distressed by the depraved conduct of the lawless (for that righteous man, living among them day after day, was tormented in his righteous soul by the lawless deeds he saw and heard)" (2 Peter 2:7-8 NIV). Both Lot and Abraham were righteous men but, there were many differences between the fruit in their lives. Abraham lived his life as a rescuer (Genesis 14) and an intercessor (Genesis 18). However, Lot lived a life of distress and torment. He only had the salvation that Paul described in 1Corinthian 3:15, "If any man's work is burned up, he will suffer loss; but he himself will be saved, yet so as through fire."

The lives of Lot and Abraham remind me of one of the parables Jesus taught about seeds planted in various places (Matthew 13:21-

23). Some seeds were sown among the thorns; some seeds sown on the good soil. More than likely, Lot had heard the Word of God from his uncle Abraham. However, the worries of the world and the deceitfulness of wealth residing in Lot may have choked out the Word. Meanwhile, Abraham heard, understood, obeyed and bore fruit a hundredfold.

One day while in my early twenties, I was reading Genesis 13. I felt the Holy Spirit whispering to me that someday, when the time comes, I should say goodbye to the "Lot" within me. God knew that I had both Lot and Abraham in my heart. Lot wanted to have both worldly wealth and success and faith in God as well. Abraham sought only God even though all he could see was wilderness. Letting go of the Lot inside of me is still an everyday struggle. I pray the Lord will pour out His Grace so that I can choose what Abraham chose.

22 FROM THE CAVE

So it was that, when God destroyed the cities of the valley, God remembered Abraham and sent Lot out of the midst of the overthrow when he overthrew the cities in which Lot had lived.
Now Lot went up out of Zoar and lived in the hills with his two daughters, for he was afraid to live in Zoar.
So he lived in a cave with his two daughters.
And the firstborn said to the younger,
"Our father is old, and there is not a man on earth to come in to us after the manner of all the earth.
Come, let us make our father drink wine, and we will lie with him, that we may preserve offspring from our father....
The firstborn bore a son and called his name Moab.
He is the father of the Moabites to this day. (Genesis 19:29-32, 37)

After God destroyed Sodom and Gomorrah, Lot and his daughters moved to a cave. They could have come back to the place where Abraham lived but they chose a place isolated from other people. If Lot had considered his two daughters who had not married yet, he might have chosen some other place so that the daughters could meet their bridegrooms. Why did Lot choose a cave? Why did the daughters choose an improper way to have offspring? These two questions came to my mind when I read Genesis 19.

The Scriptures say "he was afraid". I saw fear in Lot and his daughters. Lot was afraid of the danger in the world and his daughters were afraid of being left out of the world. Fear for these reasons is common. What if something bad or painful happens to me? Or what if other people have more success or possessions than I have and I can't "catch up"?

When we have fear, what do we usually do? I don't think that we are much different from Lot and his daughters. Either we want to stay in a psychological cave or we try to accomplish the desires we have on our own, not trusting God. I saw a veteran who had gone to a war three decades ago and came home safely but he still lived in a cave of fear. I met a woman who experienced a betrayal of her friend and shut down all other relationships, living in her cave of anger. I read from a news article about a man who was bankrupt and lived in a cave of shame.

Lot and his daughters did experience a life-saving miracle. However, the miracles do not guarantee faith in God. The people of Israel saw the ten plagues that attacked the Egyptians and the miracle of the parting of the Red Sea. Some of them still wanted to go back to Egypt when they faced difficulties in the wilderness. In the same way, most people who had seen the miracle of the five loaves of bread and two fish still left Jesus (John 6:66).

Fear is like an invisible jail. When fear seizes you, it takes away your sober mind. Out of fear, Lot did not have enough faith to believe that God could save him anywhere, all the time. Lot did not focus on the power of God even though he saw it, but instead focused on other people or the possibility of destruction. Out of fear, the daughters also did not have enough faith that God could give them families in His time and His way. They slept with their father. They never imagined that their descendants would become the Moabites and the Ammonites, who 500 years later, hired Balaam to curse the descendants of Abraham.

Two thousand years later, how were the disciples of Jesus? They heard Jesus was alive but they were afraid of the Jews and shut the doors. In the middle of their fear, Jesus came into that locked room. He said to them "Peace be with you" (John 20:19). Jesus also rebuked them for their unbelief and hardness of heart (Mark 16:14). For forty days Jesus appeared to them, teaching about the Kingdom of God. After He ascended to heaven, the Holy Spirit came down to them, and then we see that their fear was gone completely. They opened the doors and shouted out who Jesus is. This result was what Jesus promised in John 14: 26-27. *"The Holy Spirit, whom the Father will send in My name, He will teach you all things, and bring to your remembrance all that I said to you. Peace I leave with you; My peace I give to you; not as the world gives do I give to you. Do not let your heart be troubled, nor let it be fearful."*

John, who wrote the words of Jesus above, also said *"perfect love casts out fear"(1 John 4:18).* John himself had experienced the love of God that cast out the fear in him. I pray the same thing happens to me when I try to shut myself up in the cave of fear. I pray that Jesus comes into my cave and holds my hand, taking me out. Even his rebuking for my unbelief is from love, the perfect love.

23 FREEDOM

Say, therefore, to the sons of Israel, 'I am the LORD, and
I will bring you out from under the burdens of the Egyptians,
and I will deliver you from their bondage.
I will also redeem you with an outstretched arm and with great judgments.
(Exodus 6:6-7)

As He [Jesus] spoke these things, many came to believe in Him.
So Jesus was saying to those Jews who had believed Him,
"If you continue in My word, then you are truly disciples of Mine;
and you will know the truth, and the truth will make you free."
They answered Him, "We are Abraham's descendants and have never yet
been enslaved to anyone, how is it that You say, 'You will become free'?"
Jesus answered them,
"Truly, truly, I say to you, everyone who commits sin is the slave of sin.
"The slave does not remain in the house forever;
the son does remain forever.
"So if the Son makes you free, you will be free indeed.
"I know that you are Abraham's descendants; yet you seek to kill Me,
because My word has no place in you.
(John 8:30-37)

Even before I became a Christian I knew the phrase "the truth will make you free," because this phrase is the motto of a famous university in South Korea. Since coming to Austin, Texas, I have found the same phrase on a building at the University of Texas. For a long time I thought "truth" and "freedom" were academic, idealistic and abstract words: Nice words on big buildings.

Several years passed before I read this verse in the Bible again and took a more serious look at its meaning. In John 8 Jesus was talking to the Jews. For the Jews, the words "free" and "slave" were not abstract terms at all. Slavery was common in the Roman Empire. When Jesus told them "the truth will make you free" they were offended, and then angry. They knew that Jesus was telling them they were slaves.

Fifteen hundred years before Jesus came to the earth, the Jews' ancestors were slaves in Egypt. They cried out to God to deliver them from their suffering, and God himself came down to free them from slavery (Exodus 3:8). The Israelites of Moses' time knew that they were slaves. However, their descendants in Jesus' time did not recognize that they were slaves to sin. Slavery to man or slavery to sin – which slavery is stronger? I think that slavery to sin is stronger because it is more difficult to realize that we are its slaves.

Did the Israelites in Egypt listen to Moses, who spoke about God's plan to free them from slavery to the Egyptians? Not at first. Exodus 6:9 says, "Moses spoke thus to the sons of Israel, but they did not listen to Moses on account of their despondency and cruel bondage." Similarly, when their descendants heard God's plan to free them from the slavery of sin, they did not listen to Jesus either. In response to Jesus' words, the Jews repeated "Abraham is our father (v.39)." They assumed that they were free from anyone and anything just because they were the descendants of Abraham. While they were no longer slaves to other people, they were still slaves to sin. Jesus was born in order to save His people from their sins (Matthew 1:21).

The Bible says "from their sins";
it does not say "from their poverty
> illness,
>> unemployment or
>> depression."

The Jews could not to comprehend that Jesus was telling them about the slavery of sin. However, Jesus continued to tell them, perhaps with the hope that "some of them will understand when the Holy Spirit comes." Later, some of the Jews understood. The Apostle Paul explained this in Romans 6:6-7 and 14, "knowing this, that our old self was crucified with Him, in order that our body of sin might be done away with, so that we would no longer be slaves to sin for he who has died is freed from sin...For sin shall not be master over you, for you are not under law but under grace."

Jesus can save anyone from any unfortunate situation. However, Jesus knows that our primary problem, the problem responsible for all suffering, is sin. He is the truth. He will make us free from the slavery of sin.

24 JOSEPH

Joseph's story covers nearly one fourth of the entire book of Genesis. Why did Moses, the author of Genesis, write so much about this one man? Who was the first audience for this story? It was not written *to* us, even though every book in the Bible is written *for* us. Moses wrote this story to the people of Israel.

Who were the people of Israel? They were slaves in Egypt. But before becoming slaves, they were descendants or relatives of Joseph, a shepherd who became the wise prime minister of Egypt. When the Israelites became slaves, they gradually lost their confidence and identity as the people of God. I believe that Joseph's story was a big encouragement for the people of Israel, who were wondering why their lives were so miserable, painful, and unfair.

Perhaps it would be very difficult for people who were treated like scum of the earth to change their negative self-concepts. They needed something "big" to lift their spirits. They needed a story, a story like Joseph's story. He was a slave once but under God's sovereign hand, Joseph had a glorious life. Moses had to tell the Israelites who they were and why they should go back to the land of promise. He also wanted to encourage them to abandon the life style of Egypt and live a life worthy of the calling of God. At the end of Genesis, Moses put "the will of Jacob and Joseph": this father and son wanted their bodies brought back to the land they came from. Egypt was not the place where the people of Israel were supposed to dwell forever. Moses also wrote in Exodus that "they brought Joseph's body" when the Israelites left Egypt. Exodus 13:19 says, *"Moses took the bones of Joseph with him because Joseph had made the sons of Israel swear an oath. He had said, 'God will surely come to your aid, and then you must carry my bones up with you from this place'".*

For the people of Israel, Joseph's story was the reminder of what God had done for them and what God would do. God saved the family of Jacob from the seven-year drought. He provided a refuge place, Goshen, to prosper the seventy into a huge number of people, and someday God would send them back to the land He had promised to Abraham. The people of Israel could have faith through Joseph's story. They were once slaves, but they had to have faith that they would become a treasure to God (Exodus 19:5-6).

We who live in the 21st century also need a story, especially if we are poor in spirit and hunger for righteousness just like the Israelites in Egypt. We need our "Joseph", who reminds us of what our gracious God did for us in the land of wilderness so that we can be encouraged to fix our eyes on the land of promise that God will take us to. Here God gave us Someone who is greater than Joseph. His name is Jesus.

Joseph's life is like a map to guide us into the life of our Savior. We have not seen the returned Jesus yet, but we can have faith in the promise of the magnificent glory that Jesus will bring when he returns. Joseph foreshadows Jesus. Let me explain the resemblances between Joseph and Jesus.

Joseph's father, Jacob, loved him very much (Genesis 37:3). Joseph was not the first son, but Jacob seemed to regard him as the most important heir because Jacob gave him a special tunic and had him supervise his other brothers. Our Savior is the only begotten and beloved Son of God the Father. The Father has given all things into His hand (John3:35). Jesus also had a special tunic that was seamless, woven in one piece (John 19:23).

Joseph was hated, mocked, stripped of his tunic by his brothers, and then thrown into a pit (Genesis 37:4-24). Jesus was also hated by the Jewish leaders. He was mocked and stripped of his tunic by Roman soldiers.

Joseph was sold for twenty pieces of silver by his brothers (Genesis 37:28), while Jesus was sold for thirty shekels of silver by Judas, one of his disciples (Matthew 26:14-16). Both of them were betrayed by a close man.

Joseph and Jesus both experienced being humbled. Joseph once was a beloved son, and then became a slave and a prisoner (Genesis 39). Jesus left behind all the glories of heaven and came to the earth in the form of a bond-servant (Philippians 2:6-7).

Joseph was tempted by Potiphar's wife but fled (Genesis 39). Jesus was tempted by the devil in the wilderness but overcame by the Words of God (Hebrews 4:15). Both of them were falsely accused but did not sin. Potiphar's wife accused Joseph of trying to seduce her and the Jews accused Jesus of blasphemy.

The Bible says that God was with Joseph, and so he prospered even in the prison (Genesis 39:21-22). God was also with Jesus so he could heal all who were oppressed by the devil (Acts 10:38).

God exalted Joseph over the land of Egypt. He became Pharaoh's prime minister and saved the people from seven years of drought (Genesis 41 and 42). Jesus is exalted and his name is above every name (Philippians 2:8-11) after His death on the cross and His resurrection. He sits at the right hand of God.

Finally, Joseph forgave his brothers who repented of their sins toward him. Our Lord Jesus proclaimed forgiveness, too. Through his disciples we can see Jesus is still calling the people of Israel to come back to Him and be reconciled with God through Him.

Joseph's life only lasted for 110 years but our King lives forever. The story of Jesus is still in progress today. One day He will return as the King of Kings and we will see his magnificent glory.

So, as Joseph's brothers were humbled in the presence of Joseph, the prime minister of Egypt, so one day we will kneel before and worship the King of all creation. But as Joseph was tender-hearted toward his brothers, I hope to hear from my Savior the same words that Joseph told the brothers.

"Come closer to me"...
"He kissed all his brothers"...
(Genesis 45:2, 15)

25 GIVE THANKS

Now a man came from Baal-shalishah,
and brought the man of God
bread of the first fruits, twenty loaves of barley
and fresh ears of grain in his sack. And he said,
"Give them to the people that they may eat."
His attendant said,
"What, will I set this before a hundred men?"
But he said,
"Give them to the people that they may eat, for thus says the LORD,
'They shall eat and have some left over.'"
So he set it before them,
and they ate and had some left over,
according to the word of the LORD.   (II King 4: 42-44)

One day I visited a newly built building. A fresh paint smell filled the space. In the middle of the hallway, there was a miniature of the building. Architects often make such scale models when they plan new buildings. It was well made and I could see the whole structure and street view all together. In that moment I thought that many people or even things in the Old Testament are like the miniatures for the coming Savior. Elisha is one of them.

One of Elisha's stories seems like a small version of Jesus' miracle of the five loaves and two fish. In the two stories the three main characters are 1) the miracle maker who wants to feed the crowd, 2) a servant who is wondering how the smaller amount of food can satisfy the crowd, and 3) a person who dedicated the food. Both crowds were satisfied and there were even leftovers.

Since the Jews were familiar with the stories of Elisha, a great prophet who was called Man of God, they could see the miracle Jesus had performed, and then recall the story of Elisha's miracle. They would see Elisha in Jesus. No wonder the crowd said, "This is truly the Prophet who is to come into the world" (John 6: 14).

The food and the numbers of people were different. Elisha fed one hundred people with twenty loaves of bread and some grain, while Jesus fed more than five thousand people with five loaves of bread and two fish. However, the same ingredient was in both miracles.

Look at Elisha's story. There is something special about the food. The bread was made out of the first fruits and the grain was fresh. We can tell that this food was an offering from a man who wanted to express his grateful heart to God. The food was dedicated to God first in thanksgiving. Now look at Jesus' story. What did Jesus do before he distributed the food? He took the loaves and gave thanks. Giving thanks made the ordinary food into extraordinary miracles.

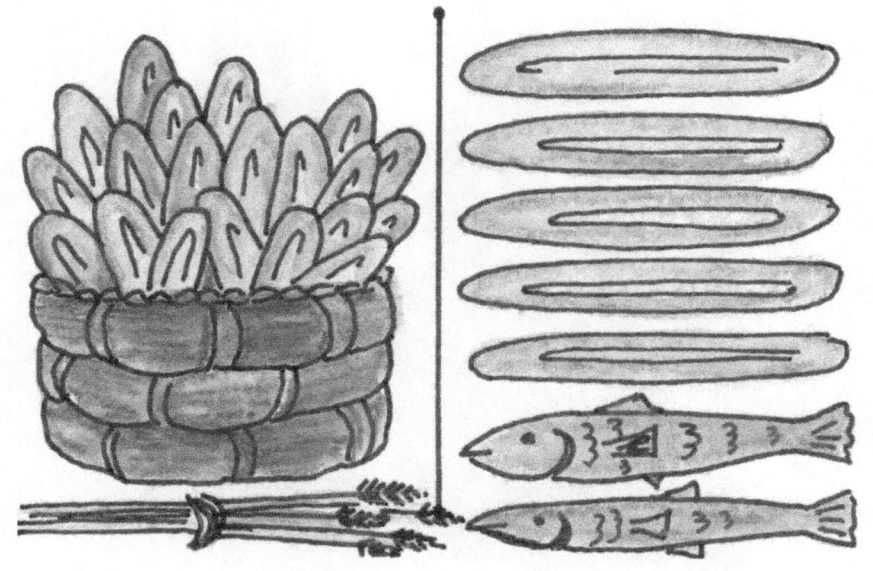

26 UP TO THE BRIM

Now a certain woman of the wives of the sons of the prophets
cried out to Elisha, "Your servant my husband is dead,
and you know that your servant feared the LORD;
and the creditor has come to take my two children to be his slaves."

Elisha said to her, "What shall I do for you? Tell me, what do you have in
the house?" And she said, "Your maidservant has nothing in the house
except a jar of oil." Then he said, "Go, borrow vessels at large for yourself
from all your neighbors, even empty vessels; do not get a few."And you
shall go in and shut the door behind you and your sons,
and pour out into all these vessels, and you shall set aside what is full."

So she went from him and shut the door behind her and her sons;
they were bringing the vessels to her and she poured. When the vessels
were full, she said to her son, "Bring me another vessel." And he said to
her, "There is not one vessel more." And the oil stopped. Then she came
and told the man of God. And he said, "Go, sell the oil and pay your debt,
and you and your sons can live on the rest." (II Kings 4:1-6)

Watching an imitation often brings us laughter and joy. Why? Maybe when we discover the similarities between the original story and the imitation, we get an "ah-hah moment" when we make the connections between the stories. We also feel a bond with others who made the same connections because they also know the original story.

I had this joy when I read some of the miracles of Elisha and found their similarities to the miracles of Jesus. Even though Elisha was born centuries before Christ and performed the miracles before Christ, I know that Jesus's miracles are the "real story" and Elisha's miracles are the "imitations." In the book of John, Chapter 2, we see the miracle Jesus performed for a wedding at Cana. The Apostle John said that the miracle was the beginning of Jesus' signs. Signs? It was not just a miracle that surprises people. It was a sign to tell them who Jesus was. If you know the stories of Elisha in the Old Testament, and read John 2, you will probably recognize the similarities between these stories of Elisha and Jesus: the oil jars of a widow and the choice wine for a wedding.

There are many similarities in these stories, but there is also one big difference. Jesus transformed water to wine, while Elisha increased the amount of oil. It seems to me that the first one is a chemical change and the other is a physical change. Of course, Jesus' miracle is more powerful. Think about the whole time period that a water drop from the clouds comes down to a vine field, permeates into the root, and comes up to the branches. Finally, grapes are formed, and then men fermented the grape juice into wine. This is a natural law. But Jesus, our Creator, could skip both natural law and man's process.

Both miracles were for a family. Both miracles were requested by women. In the Old Testament, however, the miracle was for the woman who had lost her husband In the New Testament, the miracle was for a newlywed couple who were celebrating their beginning as a family.

Both Jesus and Elisha simply "said" what to do. Elisha did not bring the jars or help fill them with oil. He just "said" to the widow. After hearing the words, it was the widow's choice to respond in faith. Jesus did the same thing. He just "said" to others. If the servants and Mary had had doubts and did not obey, the miracle would not have taken place. In both stories, the women responded in faith.

Jesus used what the wedding host family had: six stone water pots and their servants. The host did not have to buy other materials. Elisha also used what the widow had in her hands (II King 4:2): a jar of oil and her two boys. The widow and the children had to run to borrow more jars.

Borrowing jars from all the neighbors? This activity might have brought the neighbors' attention to what would happen to this poor family. And the news about the miracle by Elisha could have spread all over the town. A wedding event in the ancient time of Israel was a community party. It was open to any relatives and friends. It is no wonder that the miracle at the wedding place would spread out to the whole town.

Another thing in common is that both Jesus and Elisha ordered the workers to fill the liquid up to the brim. Elisha told the widow, fill the jars. And Jesus told the servants the same thing. John 2:7 says the servants filled the pots up to the brim. Both Jesus and Elisha also gave abundantly. Jesus gave "choice" wine, not just ordinary wine (John 2:10). The oil in jars was enough not only to pay all the debt but also to cover living costs for the family. Our God is a good God, as Paul says in Ephesians 3: 20 "He who is able to do far more abundantly beyond all that we ask or think…"

Centuries apart, on a different scale and in different situations, the two miracles have certain similarities. Why? I believe that God wanted to give us the clues about who the true Messiah is. Elisha's story helps us recognize Jesus as the Prophet of God. We also understand and interpret Jesus' story better with Elisha's story.

Lord,

When something is insufficient,
and my life become desperate for help,
I will run to you as the widow did.
I will ask you for help as Mary did.

When you simply "say" what to do,
Let me remember these two stories
so I should not be disappointed and move my legs to obey
and fill the jars that you have appointed *up to the brim*
with the substance you have ordered.

I will be happy about the miracle you will bring to me.
but I will be much happier
because I will know You better.

ABOUT THE AUTHOR

Yeonjai Rah, born in 1974 in Seoul, South Korea, moved to the U.S. in 2001. She received her Ph.D. in Educational Policy and Leadership Analysis from the University of Wisconsin-Madison in 2007. Her dream was to build a Christian school for families of diverse cultural backgrounds. To get closer to her dream she founded Bridge International Christian Academy in 2012 (bicarr.org). There are many blessings the Lord has bestowed upon her. The most precious gift was that Jesus came to her life and became her faithful Shepherd. And the Lord gave her Christian communities where she can grow and learn about Him. She lives with her husband and daughter and is grateful for these two gifts from God.

Contact: yeonjairah@gmail.com

ABOUT THE ILLUSTRATOR

Mary D. Black was born in 1966 in San Antonio, Texas. She received her BA in Art from Angelo State University in 1988. Her dream was to serve God, marry, raise her children and live her life as creatively as she could. She has been blessed with the ability to stay home to care for her children, Emily and Zachary. She is honored to serve the Lord by sharing her love of Art and talents by teaching, designing sets, murals and paintings.

Contact: contrarymarypaint@gmail.com

Her talents and interests are shared on: contrarymarypaint.blogspot.com

www.ingramcontent.com/pod-product-compliance
Lightning Source LLC
Chambersburg PA
CBHW030621070426
42449CB00041B/986